T0067126

HUMANITY HAS LOST ITS SOUL

LEON TUAM

authorHOUSE®

AuthorHouse™
1663 Liberty Drive
Bloomington, IN 47403
www.authorhouse.com
Phone: 1 (800) 839-8640

Published by AuthorHouse   03/25/2015

ISBN: 978-1-5049-0313-4 (sc)
ISBN: 978-1-5049-0312-7 (e)

Print information available on the last page.

Contents

Foreword.. vii

Dedication ix

They behave almost all like vultures..................................... 1

Trust 3

The mother and the child 4

As reward 8

We all carry and cast some nets.. 8

Woven with threads of injustice 10

Beneath the tears..14

Talking of democracy today 16

Man in public 19

Did you say 'wisdom'?...21

Visiting my grandmother 22

Humanity has lost its soul... 29

You are a very strange being 33

My African saints and prophets... 34

Prayers and actions 40

I stare, and stare at my beloved Africa 42

They are made of sweat, of blood...................................... 47

The independence of our country 49

At that very dangerous age 54

Our fights for freedom 58

Good leaders 59

Young people today... 63

Before we met 66

Dreams, dreams! 69

Water's teeth 71

Is it the twilight of humankind? 73

Money and friendship 75

Under escort, at last it penetrated Abidjan 76

In our daily life 86

The raped and the rescuer 88

Death certificates 91

Not knowing each other 96

To Enoh Meyomesse 98

As one people 101

Bushy words 102

Horse-Africa 104

The sky turned brighter 106

We became the hybrids of the changing world 110

Unsettled by my straight answer 111

It was a wonderful day 115

Story of my father and his visitors 118

I know we are all important 127

Do you see that child? 129

Life is adaptation 132

Hundreds of years after those tragedies 133

At this segment of the journey 138

Foreword

A note for the reader …

In your hands rests a rich, pleasant collection of poems which cuts across the globe. In its pages are skillfully packed wisdom and entertainment.

In a clear language and through a variety of topics, this book reminds us that the so-called fall of the old social order fed by barbarities, dictatorship and inequalities did not –Halas!— usher in a new, freer social order characterized by peace, true freedom and justice for all.

Despite all the social, economic and scientific progresses, the world lives in perpetual fears and tears. Here and there, people are wrapped in hypocrisy. We live piling and piling mountains of lies. Individuals and nations have chosen the wrong path; they have walked away from the life of integrity and dignity.

From here come most of our problems. And as injustices, duplicity and violence continue to hug and rock the world, the poet wonders if Humanity would ever regain its soul. He puts his hope in love. At the end of the day, love is what will bring together the weak and the strong, the good and the bad, the just and the unjust, etc.

In your hands rests a rich, pleasant collection of poems full of wisdom which cuts across the globe. Sip it, sip it!

Dedication

To all those hearts around the world who have lost
some loved ones in wars and violence
fuelled by greed or hate.

To all the displaced men, women and children,
due to wars and violence of all sorts.

They behave almost all like vultures

Young men and women of this land

Behave almost all like vultures.

They love the easy life,

They love to live well,

They love and enjoy material goods,

But they hate to roll up their sleeves.

Young men and women of this land

Behave almost all like vultures.

They love good things,

They love the good life,

But they hate to bend their backs.

Ah, young men and women of this land!

Young men and women of this land

Behave almost all like vultures.

They love easy things,

But they hate to bend their backs.

They love easy things,

But they hate effort and endurance.

Ah, young men and women of this land!

They curse virtue, they ignore virtue,

They rebuff virtue, they banish virtue,

But they search and woo all sorts of vices,

They ecstatically hug all sorts of vices.
Ah, young men and women of this land!

They sniff everywhere at easy life,
They scent and track the easy meal
Like a swarm of vultures which always
Know how to be on time on a fallen game.
Ah, young men and women of this land!

With vultures-men and vultures-women,
Ah! How would this land go up?
Go up and up without making bad stops?
If only our great grandparents
Could come in flesh and witness all this?

Young men and women of this land
Behave almost all like vultures.

There have always been disasters,
There have always been disasters;
But the big disaster comes upon a people
As their future makes a U turn.
Ah my land! Ah my beloved land!

Trust

You say that trust comes first.
You stress that trust comes first.
I've walked warily in the book of life.
I've read a lot from the world book of life.
You say that I must trust you.
You stress that I must trust you.

To trust …
Ah to trust!
To trust isn't indeed an easy thing.
To trust someone's the toughest of things.
Am I not right? (Silence)
Isn't true? (Silence)

You say, Trust!
To trust, to trust isn't an easy thing.
You eagerly want me to trust you.
But how can I easily trust you
When at times I've failed to trust myself?
To trust, to trust isn't an easy thing.

The mother and the child

By a nice fire
On the mother's limbs
In a blooming evening,
The child fights,
The child grumbles,
The child whines.

The child fights,
The child fights, fights and fights.
Against an invisible enemy fights the child.
The child grumbles,
The child whines.

And the mother sings,
Sings some soft creamy songs,
In order to disarm the little soldier:
The mother sings,
Sings some springy sugared songs
In order to appease the fighter.

On the mother's limbs
By a nice fire
In a blooming evening,
The child cries,
Cries and cries.

The mother sings and sings.

The child cries, cries and cries.

The mother shows that she knows her job,

She sings and smiles,

She sings sings and sings.

The mother stirs the legs,

Gently the mother shakes the legs

And sings, sings to rock the fighting child.

The child fights the invisible enemy,

The child cries, cries and cries.

The mother stirs the legs,

The mother shakes the legs

And sings, similes; sings and sings.

The child cries …

The child fights,

Fights against the invisible enemy.

The mother shows that she knows her job,

The mother clings onto her songs,

The mother remains nice and smiles,

The mother sings, sings and sings.

The child's voice weakens,

The mother gently shakes the legs

And sings; sings, ardently sings.

The child's voice sinks.

The mother sings, sings ardently,
And the child sinks,
Slowly sinks, sinks,
Sinks deeply into the sleep,
Sinks deeply into the sleep,
And the mother into the silence.

She's sweating a little on the face.
She looks at her child.
Her curious eyes fly
And land on the child face.

Like the morning steam
That rises from the water,
She views innocence
And grace gush from it.

She cannot believe that the storm
That shakes her comes
From the tiny creature;
She mutters:

Sleep, sleep my baby.
Sleep; sleep, my quiet water.
But you are deep, deeper.

You are feeble and vulnerable,
But you are wild-fierce,
You are very strong.

You can hurt,
You can even kill.

Yes at this age, child,
You can mortally hurt.
My child, my child,
You can kill easily.

And today when I look around,
When I view all these young people
Venture on this way without any experience,
I feel frightened,
I pity them; I pity children like you.

My child, my beloved child,
You can kill, you can easily kill.
And with those children-parents out there,
I feel deeply sad for children like you.

O vulnerable strong creature, sleep!
In any being is concealed a big mystery.
In any being hides a volcano.
Any being is a volcano.
We are all sleepy volcanoes.

Sleep, sleep my baby;
Sleep, my innocent child, sleep!
Sleep, O my quiet deep water!

As reward

Once I helped a man and he appreciated it so much.
He used to play and have a lot of fun with his pet.
But it happened that that pet-reptile could barely move.
Sadness and bitterness took control of his whole life.

I treated his pet, and he went back to happy life.
He was so happy, and appreciated it so much.
As reward, he used his pet to break my heart.
As reward, he used his pet to shred my peaceful hearth.
Once I helped a man and he appreciated it so much.

We all carry and cast some nets

We all carry and cast some nets,
And we are all caught in the nets.

Tears at times are nets,
Smile and laughter are nets,
Gestures at times are nets,
Words are nets,
Even our nicest acts can be nets,
They can just be hidden ladders.

Tears, smile and laughter are nothing
When they mean something else.
Gestures, words and acts are nothing
When they mean something else.

We're naturally armed,
Armed with soft, fatal nets,
Armed to wound lives and to be wounded.
We carry and cast many nets,
And in the nets we are caught, too.

Tears,
Smile,
Laughter,
Gestures,
And
Words are our Ring of Gyges.
They are our best camouflage,
They are our preferred pistols,
They found our might.

We all carry and cast nets,
And we are all caught in the nets.

Woven with threads of injustice

In this country,

This beautiful country,

This land where a handful of barbarians

Hold all the country's Strength

And keep the people in the cave of ignorance,

And keep them in the lower valley of anguish,

And keep them in the throes of want and death,

In this country,

This beautiful country,

This land where a handful of barbarians

Master the art of putting the people to sleep,

It is said that justice's for all,

It is said that justice's for all,

And the people swallow it,

Ah and the people eagerly swallow it.

The people swallow this opium…

Oh, yes! They do.

In this country,

This beautiful country,

This land where a handful of barbarians

Own all the Lungs of the nation,

In this rich looted stained country,
Life is woven with threads of injustice still.

In this country,
This beautiful country,
The people want to dream big,
The people want to dream bigger.
Alas, the ceiling of their dreams is too short,
And they end up dreaming small, smaller.
As the ceiling of their dreams
Comes down, comes down and keeps
Coming down, coming down, down…
The people end up living dreamlessly,
Living dreamlessly, ah dreamlessly!

But in this country,
This beautiful country,
Barbarians' dreams don't have any ceiling,
Like strong strange sky rockets, their dreams
Move majestically faster, louder, farther
And enter the firmament to tour it forever.
There isn't any ceiling for these vermin's dreams,
Their ceiling does not exist, it does not exist.
They soar, they soar like Daedalus,
They are high, they are high with greed.
They dream, they dream big,
They dream, they dream bigger…
They dream bigger, they dream humongous.

In this country,

This beautiful country,

Life is woven with threads of injustice still.

But we expect some great days.

It is dark still, but there will be light here.

No doubt, there will be light,

The people will see the light here,

There will be light, there will be light here.

The people will touch and taste the light.

In this country,

This beautiful country,

The people will push the barbarians,

The people will push, push the barbarians

And they'll fall down, and fall to pieces

As jailed justice breaks the boulders,

As jailed justice grinds and grinds the boulders.

In this country,

This beautiful country,

As jailed justice will break the boulders

And kiss the forehead of this country,

Life will be so beautiful, so beautiful.

Life will be the fresh flesh of the mango

That gives the tongue a lascivious pleasure.

In this country,
This beautiful country,
When justice will break the boulders,
When justice will break the boulders
And kiss the cheeks of this country,

Life will be so beautiful, so beautiful.
Life will be the fresh flesh of the mango
That speaks unctuously to the mouth,
That speaks bewitchingly to the teeth.

It's indeed the future life of this country,
It's the future of this rotten country
That's woven with steely threads of injustice.
In this country,
This beautiful country,
Life will be beautiful, so beautiful.

Beneath the tears

I remember when that tongue spat:
After all that has happened,
I have my tears left to cling on.

And I said:
No, it's not the essence of human.
It does not look like us, such a choice.
That resort is a peril to the society.

We talked and talked and I concluded:

Now you believe that on earth
All what you have left are your tears.
Let them come. Let them stream.

Let the tears come. Let them stream.
But hasten, hasten to stop those tears.
Let the tears come. Let them stream,
Let them be a heavy but short rain.

And be very careful; when frustration
And anger devour us, with a machete
We can mow our ears warding off a fly.

Life is a big thing, life is a huge thing.
Life is a very serious matter to give up on.
Nothing, nothing on earth should come
(Like a thief who picks our belongings)
And grab our life and take it away.

Be very careful! In the deep night,
Our own hands can firmly grasp
And press a mamba against our own body.

Oh let those tears come. Let them go.
Beneath those tears, those heavy tears,
Beneath those tears, those stormy tears;
There is the brightest of days.

Let your tears stream. Let them stream.
I say, let them stream, let them stream…
But day by day, do your best to get stronger.
Like someone who dries the seawater
To get at last the pure salt,
O, dry your tears to collect the salt of life.

Talking of democracy today

Democracy, democracy, democracy …
Everywhere they talk of democracy.
Every time I hear the word 'Democracy',
I jump, I jump and jump with fright.
Every time I hear the word 'Democracy',
My heart beats fast, my heart beats faster.
Democracy, democracy, democracy …

I have seen terrible things under democracy.
I have seen dreadful poverties under democracy,
I have seen haunting tragedies under democracy.
Democracy's a hollow word.
Democracy's a deceitful word.
Democracy, democracy, democracy …

People easily get high on democracy,
While injustices suck them, suck them to marrow.
While democracy caresses and rocks the people,
While democracy anaesthetizes the people,
Injustices of all sorts suck them, suck them softly,
Suck them silently; suck them, suck them caressingly,
And turn them in the end into zombies,
And turn them in the end into zombies.
Democracy, democracy, democracy …

Every time I hear the word 'Democracy',
I jump, I jump and jump of fright.
Every time I hear the word 'Democracy',
My heart beats fast, my heart beats faster.
Democracy, democracy, democracy …

Democracy's a huge, light pleasant ball
Which politicians have mastered the art of playing with.
They have mastered the art of playing with
To score and score and score against the people,
Making sure that the people don't see the comic part of it.
Politicians have mastered the art of kicking it very well.
They know how to use it against the people,
They know how to use it to protect the wealthy,
They know how to use it to improve their own lives,
They know how to use it to control the people.
Democracy, democracy, democracy …

Justice to politicians is a small heavier mass.
They are always very afraid of it,
They know it can quickly smash them mortally.
To wrap politicians into a thick uneasiness,
One must talk to them about wounded justice,
And show them injustices' deep injuries on the people.
To get politicians out of the wrap, out of the coma,
To make them feel better and better,
To chase the dark cloud away from their faces,
Talk of democracy; just go back to democracy.
Democracy, democracy, democracy …

O people!
Let us talk less and less of democracy,
Let us talk less and less of democracy,
And take good care of justice,
And take good care of justice.

When justice's served,
Debate about democracy's useless.
When justice's served,
Debate about democracy crumbles down.
When justice's served,
Democracy's useless.
Democracy, democracy, democracy …

Man in public

In our society, deep in our society,
Man in public might say to all
Or show to all he is woman's superior.
Indeed, he says and shows that he is.
He shows it, he says it very often.

As they hear or see this go on,
The wise of our society just smile.
They know all, they know all those lies.
They know those lies and just smile.
Ah they stealthily look at that and laugh.

Man in public might humiliate the woman
But the wise of our society know all,
They know all.
Weak or silly as she might appear,
Woman is man's stick.
And the wise of our society know it.

If this stick ever falls down,
If this stick ever falls down, really falls down,
Man's nobility would be in jeopardy.
Man's indignity would be seen even by the blind.
And the wise of our society know it.

Man might think he is woman's superior.

But the wise of our society know all,

They know all.

Weak or silly as she might appear,

Woman is the belt that holds man's G-string.

And the wise of our society know it.

If this belt ever cuts off,

If this belt ever cuts off, really cuts off,

Man's intimacy would become a roofless house,

Man's nakedness would be seen even by the blind.

And the wise of our society know it.

In our society, silently in our silent society,

These thoughts flow on the Wise's tongues

Like a powerful stream through the forest.

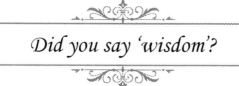

Did you say 'wisdom'?

Did you say 'wisdom'?
I love wisdom and would like to be wise.
The desire of being wise is a fire on my soul.

The desire of being wise is a rebellious
Doughty palm wine in my heart:
It ferments, it froths and overflows.

Wisdom to me is what water's to life.
I love wisdom and would like to be wise,
And would like to live and die wise,
But not sleepily stupidly wise.
I hate and scorn any soporific wisdom.

Amid the frustrations of our people,
Amid the humiliations of our people,
I hate the naivety and cowardice
Of our leaders that are often seen as wisdom,
I hate, I execrate the wisdom of doom.

I love wisdom; wisdom is life's fertilizer.
I love wisdom, I do love it, I venerate it.
But I hate, I execrate any handcuff-wisdom.
Always I abhor seeing people
Engulf it or be fed on; I do, Oh I do.

Visiting my grandmother

My grandmother opens it and says,
Come in, welcome, son; welcome.

On her face raises and flourishes a big light.
I give her a parcel and while I sit down,
She laughs. She laughs, ah, ah, ah.
Welcome, son. Welcome, ah, ha, ha …

I look down and say,
My dear mother,
You never welcome me with laughter;
My dear mother, what does this mean?
What's happening, dear mother?

She says: son,
I am just happy. I am back from the city.
I went to the city last week,
I visited my grandchildren and their mother.

Son, she is a lady's pencil.
She knows how to hold the pencil.
She knows it very well.
She can hold it to fill a house with money.
She has two children, only two.

She has a beautiful big house.
I love her big, big backyard, son.
Son, I love it, I love it.
She does not grow any food on it.
She does not have on it any henhouse.
It has the lawn and around it some flowers.

I begged her to go and buy some hens
I could spend time feeding,
But she said, no, no. I cannot do that.
They'd make the lawn dirty,
They'd dig and fill it with holes.

But every morning before leaving,
She puts the water for all sorts of birds.
The birds come and drink and fight,
They come and drink and chat,
They come and drink and sing,
They quench their thirst and count stories,
They quench their thirst and play.

Those birds come and drink and bathe,
They drink, they chat, they sing,
They bathe, they play,
But also they fight against death
They don't forget that they have
To have many, many babies after all.

In the backyard, those birds think about it,
And openly they do something about it.
They do it. They do it all day.
They drink. They chat, they sing and play,
And they do something about it.
They do it all day, all day long.

She has two children, only two.
She has a lot of food,
Different kinds of food,
And some of them are strange,
Very odd, O son!
They may even come from heaven.
But she has two children, only two.

Before I left, we sat down
And I talked to her. I told her the truth.
I looked into her eyes and said:

You are a lady's pencil.
You hold a long, long pencil.
You know how to hold the pencil,
And it is good.
You have a lot of foods, good foods,
And it's good.

But you have a problem.
You have enough goods,
(To dare say you have a good fortune
May incite the gods to split

And share with those who have less)
All for a meager number of children.
No, no, no… work on it.

And you have a big problem.
You do not grow foods here,
You do not grow foods here,
Even a single banana plant,
Because you do not know how to,
And do not want to.

You do not breed animals here,
Even a single pigeon,
A single one for the worst of days,
Because you do not know how to,
Because you do not understand life,
And do not want to, not want to, at all.

You turn that thing over there
And the water comes out, sheee… sheeee!
You collect the amount you want
And turn the thing to silence it.

You cannot go and get some water
From the public fountain,
Or from the public well,
Or from the river and boil it.
You do not know where they are,
You do not know how it works,
And you are not ready to try.

You do not use the firewood
To cook or warm the house,
Because you do not know how to,
Because you do not know where to fetch it,
And do not want to.

You turn that massive steel,
It breathes, breathes noisily
And stretches its burning cruel tongue;
You put your food on it and, quick,
It is ready and you eat.

It is cold, you press that thing,
And it spits the heat.
It is hot; you press that other thing,
And it casts its cold breath around.

In that cold coffin put up
That is fed with electri...ty,
You keep cold and perishable foods.
It is your way and the unique here.
That cold coffin is all you have as loft.

If you go to the market tomorrow
To buy food and find nobody,
The next day and find nobody, or no food,
The following, and the next, no food,
If you go next week and the following
And find nobody, no food:
Would you go home and eat your money?

If the water stop running here and around
Today, tomorrow and the following days,
The following week, weeks, months:
Would you stay home and drink your money?

If there is no electri...ty nor gas here today,
Tomorrow and the following days,
And weeks and months:
Would you stay home and burn your money
To cook, and burn your money
To warm up or keep your food safe?
Ah what a humankind's downfall!

You are a lady's pencil.
You hold a long, long pencil.
You know how to hold the pencil,
And it's good.

But for survival sake,
To be a really educated person,
To be ready to respond and prevail
In case of bad change –you never know,
You must try everything you can,
You must learn to walk on many ways.

At the first worse social change,
You may go deeper into misery's belly,
And never shall you recover.

The pencil has given you a lot.
But given you all that,
It has stolen a lot from you, a lot.
My daughter, a lot, a lot …

Stop living like a half human.
Start living fully, thinking, thinking.
Start living fully, acting, acting
Your unwise conduct can simply
Lead you to the endless harmattan of life.
Your unwise way of life can easily
Lead you to the Bermuda of life.

As she finishes, I say to her:
Grandmother, O my mother,
I wonder: Would she change? Would she?
As I know, the city has a lot of tears,
But truly it has no ears.
Fake smiles or fake joys soak up
Or collect and store the city's tears.

As I know, the city has a lot of tears,
But truly it has no ears.
The city's the city.
When it's good there, it is good.
When it's bad there, it gets worse.

Humanity has lost its soul

When we look at what is going on now,
When we look at what is going on now,
We perceive that liberty's still too far.
We perceive that liberty's still too far.
Oh, against the weak works the world!
Against the poor works the world!
Oh humanity!
Humanity has lost its soul.

When we look at what is going on now,
When we look at what is going on now,
We notice that freedom is still away.
We notice that freedom is still away.
Oh, against the weak works the world!
Against the poor works the world!
Oh humanity!
Humanity has lost its soul.

When we look at what is going on now,
When we look at what is going on now,
We see that the skyline is full of dreads.
We see that the skyline is full of dreads.
Oh, against the weak works the world!
Against the poor works the world.
Oh humanity!
Humanity has lost its soul.

When we look at what is going on now,

When we look at what is going on now,

We come across of a new long journey.

We come across of a new long journey.

Oh, against the weak works the world!

Against the poor works the world.

Oh humanity!

Humanity has lost its soul.

When we look at what is going on now,

When we look at what is going on now,

Tears form, tears gush and besiege our eyes.

Oh, against the weak works the world!

Against the poor works the world.

Oh humanity!

Humanity has lost its soul.

When we look at what is going on now,

When we look at what is going on now,

Deep sorrow builds its fortress in our chest.

Deep sorrow builds its fortress in our chest.

Oh, against the weak works the world!

Against the poor works the world.

Humanity has lost its soul.

When we look at what is going on now,

When we look at what is going on now,

Despair, fear and pain take refuge in us.

Despair, fear and pain take refuge in us.

Oh, against the weak works the world!

Against the poor works the world.
Oh humanity!
Humanity has lost its soul.

Many filthy things; many conspiracies,
Many, many wars; many useless wars.
Nasty wars and bloodsheds here and there,
They're wars and bloodsheds driven by greed.
People live and work together,
They share many things together,
But they are totally wrapped in loneliness.
New diseases spread and kill and kill …
And they all are questionable diseases.
Oh, against the weak works the world!
Against the poor works the world.
Oh humanity!
Humanity has lost its soul.

Here, there and over there,
The story of nations remains the same.
Here, there and over there,
A handful of thugs smile and pile mounts of lies,
They smile and pile lies and pile them high.
They bite into people's rights and lives,
And smiling they pile lies and pile them higher,
They smile and pile and pile them highest.
They pile lies and pile lies and pile lies.
And people believe, and believe them.
Oh, against the weak works the world!
Against the poor works the world.

Oh humanity!
Humanity has lost its soul.

Here, there and over there,
A handful of thugs have jailed the Earth.
Here, there and over there,
In many ways our world has failed,
Our world has failed in many ways,
In many ways, in many ways it's failed,
Except in the exercise of cruelty,
Except in the exercise of cruelty.
And people live in anger and fear,
Everywhere people live in anger and fear.
Oh, against the weak works the world!
Against the poor works the world.
Oh humanity!
Humanity has lost its soul.

When we look at what is going on now,
When we look at what is going on now,
Peace and all hope fly away from us,
Distress and great pain take refuge in us.
Oh, against the weak works the world!
Against the poor works the world.
Oh humanity!
Humanity has lost its soul.

Humanity has lost its soul,
Humanity has lost its soul.
Hm hm hm hm hm hm hm hm!
Hm hm hm hm hm hm hm hm!

You are a very strange being

You plunge into the fresh water,
You play and play with it.
You swim and swim across it.
You wander and wander in it.
And as you get out of it,
You say a very strange thing,
You say an amazing thing, yes!
You state that you are dying from thirst.

Thrown into a pond filled with palm oil,
You sojourn in it and come out empty.
You walk away with no single drop of oil on you.
You walk away empty, dry; dry, dry.
And you start asking for cooking oil.

You are very dirty and you are stinking.
A calabash of water breaks onto your head,
The water runs down until the container's empty.
But you remain dirty. You are still stinking.
And you start asking for water to bathe.

Ah, what can people expect from you?
What can you do? Where can you fit?
You cannot do anything for yourself,
What can you do for these people?
Tell me, what kind of person are you?
Ah a very strange being you are.

My African saints and prophets

I had many, many of them
Before African lands started
Collecting the strangers' footprints,
I had many, many saints and prophets.

I had many, many of them.
In Africa, my saints and prophets
Were birds' nests on a big plantation.

I had many saints and prophets before
Strangers stepped and settled down in Africa.
I had many, many of them.
In Africa, my saints and prophets
Outnumbered the African watercourses.

When strangers reached Africa,
I had many saints and prophets still.
I had many holy men here and there,
I had God's messengers everywhere.
I had prophets and forerunners there.

My prophets would nightly gather
Devine messages and hand them over,
Hand them over to the rulers in the morning,
Hand them over to the people in the evening.

They lived and acted for the gods and God.
They lived to carry out gods' and God's will.
They would foresee the future,
They would ask, would receive
And release good and sad omens.

During the day, my prophets would receive
Celestial messages; they would blow flutes,
They would blow trumpets to praise the Lord,
And get more messages from divinities,
And get more messages from the ancestors.

Settled down about the watercourses or waterfalls,
Settled about the lakes or on top of the mountains,
Settled amid the urban and rural populations,
They would play instruments to praise
Or interrogate the gods and ancestors,

They would look in the sky and dance,
They would look on the ground and smile,
They would close their eyes and clap,
They would look into the water and chant,
And come back with interesting messages.

From the horn of Somalia to Dakar shore,
From the Cape to the shore of Tunisia,
My saints and prophets outnumbered
The African rivers and streams and brooks.

Before the strangers' footprints kissed my lands,
Before we knew about their saints,
Before we knew about their prophets,
My Africa was full of saints and prophets.

The strangers came and were welcome.
The strangers came and discovered my religions.
These strangers denied my saints their holiness.
These strangers said my prophets
Were but on satanic missions.

They banned my religions and cultures,
They sullied and rejected my saints.
They arrested, they tortured, they deported,
They imprisoned and killed my prophets.

The strangers sullied and rejected my saints,
The strangers tortured and discarded my prophets.
Everywhere they went,
They were welcome.
Everywhere they went, they spat on us,
They desecrated our values our societies.

How could they accept my saints and prophets?
How could they respect my saints and prophets?
Ah, ah how could the strangers bow before my saints
And prophets when my African brothers and sisters
Had refused to resolutely lift them up themselves?

As the strangers talked unctuously
About their own saints and prophets,
Or talked holding a stick or a fire-eater steel,
Africans rushed like the moths called by the light,
And blindly embraced the strangers' saints,
Embraced them strongly, embraced them firmly
And got completely drunk, got drunk on naivety,
And warmly, they worshiped alien prophets.

They hugged and welcomed and housed
The strangers' saints and prophets,
Pushing mine down,
Leaving mine down, down, down…
Pulling mine in the mud, deep in the mud,
Throwing mine in the rubbish of history,
Throwing them there, throwing them far there,
O leaving them there, keeping them there!

As the strangers' lights entered Africa,
Darkness, deep darkness entered my Africa,
Darkness started veiling the face of my continent.

As the strangers' lights entered Africa,
Willingly or not, Africans embraced them.
Embracing them, they went far,
Too far, at the point that the lights' owners
Were astonished and from the Africans,
They could learn to love the lights they brought.

Who were African people?
Who are African people?
African people were the moths.
African people are the moths.
Blinded,
Devoted,
Mesmerized,
Naïve,
They rushed into the foreign lights
And got burned; they rushed and got burned,
They severely got burned.
Today, they rush into the foreign lights
And get burned; they rush and get burned,
They severely get burned still. Alas, alas.

I had saints and prophets in Africa.
I had had many, many saints and prophets,
But my African brothers and sisters
Do not appreciate again or never appreciated
What they have or had; they do not.
They do not valorize what they have.

Taken as a group,
African people exist like ghosts,
Taken as a group in the world,
African people's presence is like ghosts existence.
With their phantom presence everywhere,
African people are absent or always behind.

African people do not hold tight what they have.
And today, our saints and prophets are nowhere.
They are nowhere to be found.
Alas, they're no more, they're simply no more!
African people do not hold tight what they have.

In Africa, we have sandy golden lands
With bellies full of raw natural seeds,

In Africa, we have yellow and green lands
With fertile skins and rich stomachs,

In Africa, we have many big watercourses
And oceans whose beds are full of treasures,

In Africa, we have everything, everything.
But we do not really hold anything.
We do not hold anything tight.
And thought we are very, very rich,
We remain the poorest on earth.

And as this African reality grows
And grows thicker and bigger today,
Two Niles found their sources on my face.
Two Niles trace their courses on my face.

Nothing in Africa belongs to African people yet.
African people do not hold tight what they have.
African people, where are my saints and prophets?
African people, when should we grow up?

Prayers and actions

What we win and cherish in our life
Should foremost be spiritually sought,
Be spiritually hunted and spiritually won.

African,
Sow some prayers in the ears of your ancestors,
Sow some prayers in the ears of your gods,
Sow them in those of the great God,
And keep your limbs in motion.

Oh, don't sow your holy seeds and fold your arms.
Don't win the first battle and fold your arms.
Prayers are solely the fights for invisible victories,
Invisible victories arm us with confidence and blessing.
Solely our actions carry us to concrete victories.

African,
Prayers are the fuel and peoples are vehicles.
Prayers are the fuel for vehicles that are ready,
Prayers are fuel for vehicles in motion or ready to go.
Regrettably, in our societies, after lies and lies,
There is more fuel than vehicles that are ready.
A lot of vehicles are over fuelled and remain broken.
To play good roles, they must be repaired.

African,
This world is a big jungle,
This world is a very dark big jungle.
The one who prays and stays still
Is but an unarmed hunter cornered,
And surrounded by wild ferocious beats.
Any person who undertakes hunting
Ignoring the spiritual battle,
Solely is a blind hunter who can
Burn the entire bush to ashes.
Our prayers must always be followed by actions.
Our actions must at times be escorted by prayers.

No matter what our faith and religion,
No matter what our spiritual life,
Unless we tightly hold both lives,
Nothing significant, nothing appealing,
Nothing superior or uplifting and everlasting
Ever shall come into our life or amid us.

I stare, and stare at my beloved Africa

I stare, and stare at my beloved Africa.
I see my huge Africa shiver with tiredness,

I see my beautiful Africa totter
Like a big drunkard that cannot go far
Before falling down,

I view my Africa dance epileptically
To an inaudible music,

I look around; I look beyond and all over,
I see misery fall from children's faces
Like sweat from a great marathon runner,

I look around; I look beyond and all over,
I see despair dance on the youth's faces
Like worms that savor a carrion,

I look around; I look beyond and all over,
I hear frustrations stream on workers' tongues
Like autumnal leaves from the trees,
Or monkeys which fly over the forest,

I look around; I look beyond and all over,
I see sufferings roll in the parents' eyes

Like a big tornado in the sky,
Ready to hit the ground,

I stare, and stare at my huge Africa,
And find the origin of her uneasiness.

My Africa is a victim of abundant fruits,
My Africa is weighed down with fruits,
My Africa is collapsing under
The abundant fruits she bears,

For her sons and daughters fail
To sustaining her with strong posts,
For her sons and daughters are busy,
And busy with the wrong fights,

For her sons and daughters stand
And show strength solely in divisions,
Show strength solely in treason,
Show great strength in self-destruction;
She'd not move far; she'd just collapse.

And at last here you are, my Africa:
Neglected,
Humiliated,
Sacrificed,
Desecrated,
And slaughtered,

And here you are, my Africa:
Slaughtered,
Slaughtered by your sons and daughters,
Slaughtered with your sons and daughters,
Slaughtered with their blessings,
O my Africa, here you are,
Here you are, ah my beautiful Africa.

This is Africa we have on hands,
This is Africa we have to turn
Into a place of dream comes true;

This is Africa we have on hands,
This is Africa we have to turn
Into a place of peace,
Of smile,
And hope,
And fulfillment; this is it.

I, son of this beloved Land, promise:
Knowing that our enemy number one is Fear,
I will enable men-dogs-tails under the bellies
And women-dogs-tails under the bellies
Of this Land to be brave and great fighters
Like the nursing elephants.

I will grow food in abundance
For the famished mouths of this Land,
I will give shape to the shapelessness,
I will give peace to the unrest,

I will let justice enter this Land
And invade houses like a severe flood,
I will give true hope to the hopeless.

And you, sitting there looking
As if this land's transformation were just
The business of some Africans,
Stand up and work harder and harder.
As Bob loved to say,
Stand up and fight, or else perish.

And you, who are already at work,
You can do better, you can do better,
Be very ambitious and confident.

And you, who lack determination
And act assailed with doubts,
And act shivering with fear,
You will never go far.
Change, ah yes, change.
Nothing great on this Land
Can ever come from fearful hands.

And you, I am talking to you,
Yes you, you,
Tell what you'll do for this Africa,
Convince us of what you can do better for her.

And you, who are getting busy
Without being busy,

Be serious,

Make your pledge,

Make your pledge here now, now.

And above all, assure us that

On this vast Land of Nkrumah,

Assure us that on this vast Land of Um Nyobé,

Assure us that on this vast Land of Lumumba,

Of Gadhafi, of Sankara, of Amilcar Cabral …

Never shall you be the crack by which

The enemies might enter and damage her.

Assure us, assure us!

O let us fight all together for Africa!

African people let us not give up the fight.

Let us hang on. Let us hang on like death.

True respects never are free gifts.

We must work hard for; we must fight harder for.

True respects for us from the others come from us.

Let us fight all together for our Mother,

Yes, let us fight together for her; together, together.

They are made of sweat, of blood

Do you view?

Do you view those strong businesses?

Do you view?

Do you view these bright and rich cities?

Do you view?

Do you view these good things and places?

Do you view?

Do you view those splendid buildings?

Do you view?

Do you view these and those wealthy families?

Do you view?

Do you view all these things and those ones

That our people would like to enjoy but cannot?

Do you view them? Do you view them all?

They are made of sweat, of blood.

They are the sweat,

They are the blood.

They are the sweat of our poor people,

They are the blood of our poor people.

They are our sweat, our blood.

But the true dialogue to fix all that is rejected,

And access to our full rights is hard, harder...

And often, it seems even impossible.

Do you, do you view all of them?

We can turn our back to them and walk away.

But walk to where?
We can turn our back to them and work.
But work to get where?

There is a problem here.
There is a big problem here.
Surrounded by i,
To walk takes us nowhere.
Surrounded by i,
To work keeps us in the same conditions.

We are strong, we are capable.
Here we need j,
We just need j to blossom like flowers.
Here we need j,
We just need j to work and get better.

But to get j,
We need to crush our doubts,
We need to crush our fears,
We need to organize,
We need to build confidence,
And cultivate togetherness,
Then we need to stand up,
We need to stand up,
Stand up firmly; firmly, firmly.
It is the key to miracles,
We are miracles.
Do you understand?
Do you understand?

The independence of our country

Last year,
The authorities of our country invited the people
and mingled with them on the independence day.

Soon we will celebrate it again,
and next year and the years to come,
our authorities will invite us to celebrate it.

Our authorities will vaunt the country's progress,
they will vaunt and vaunt the milestone
that they say and believe we have made,
they will trumpet that the country's on the best path.

Soon it is our independence day and our authorities
will tell the people how blessed they are
to having good leaders that care like them,

Soon it is our independence day,
And they will roared and thundered
In the conferences rooms,
at the open-air,
over the radios,
over the TVs,
and all the mass medias
that we are at the right side of the history.

Soon it is our independence day assert
and they will tell the people how blessed they are
to living in such a peaceful blessed country.

'A blessed country', they stress.
'A blessed people', they state.
No, not the people;
The blessed ones are these authorities.

Independence without drinking water,
independence amid cholera's multiple blows,
independence rocked by monster malaria,
independence harmed by guinea worm,
No, these authorities are the blessed ones.

Independence without decent hospitals,
independence amid the rainforest
of a broken education system,
independence chained to violence and diseases,
No, these authorities are the blessed ones.

independence of a country with an army
that cannot defend our land successfully,
an army that cannot conduct and win a war,
an army that cannot protect our boundaries,
an army that cannot defend our sovereignty,
No, these authorities are the blessed ones.

Independence without electricity,
independence without a good defense system,
independence in the extreme and abject poverty.
And amid this chaos,

Our authorities live the stars' lifestyle,
and lie and despise their people,
and the people don't seize them
and chop their heads one by one;
they do all these, they act cruelly,
and nothing happens to them.
No, these authorities are the blessed ones.

Nothing happens to these life-takers,
these hopes' killers, these dreams' killers.
nothing, nothing happens to them; nothing.
No, these authorities are the blessed ones.

Stripped of our right to choose our leaders,
Stripped of our wealth and dignity,
Stripped of all our rights;

We warm up with the words
of peace, of wisdom and kindness.

Stripped of all our rights ... all our rights,
we put on the clothes of hope and love
and smile at our enemies.

We smile.
We don't want to go ahead
and do the right thing.
we smile.

Music players,
drumbeats,
xylophones' cries,
good music, good songs,
dancers,
foods,
alcohols, sex,
drogues,
cigarettes or tobaccos,
smiles, laughter …

We are a sunken people in joy.
we are a sunken people,
we keep living; we keep walking,
walking sustained by the crutches of hope.
We are a sunken people in joy.

We don't want to go ahead
and do the right thing;
many things remain hidden under our tongues
like grains under the ground
awaiting the rain;

we don't quite say what we think.
we smile as some waves of tears rock our eyes,
we laugh, we smile, smile, smile …

But even our dogs and livestock
in their daily conversations scorn us,
they scorn us and say
we are drunk over fear and cowardice.

Independence? O poor independence!
soon we will celebrate you,
and next year and the years to come.

Last year, our authorities invited us
to celebrate our pale independence,
to celebrate our scrawny independence.

this year we will celebrate it again.
country, motherland, it is all our fault.
country, motherland, we feel guilty.
We feel guilty.

Country, we simply reify ourselves daily,
country, we mulishly belittle you daily.
Country, motherland, we feel guilty.
we are guilty, we are guilty.

At that very dangerous age

I saw her walking fast,
Fast like one that is late to a big business.
I saw her walking fast,
Fast like a caterpillar that crosses a warm place.

The prairie on her head was young and thick.
Like a glass, her silky forehead was shining,
Her eyes were two pieces of diamond,
And a skeletal sun toured her face.

At the edge of her silky door,
There was a thick attractive painting
That could betray or show all those she'd kiss.

Behind her door,
Some twinkling white appealing stones
Could be seen as her soul was lit.

Her finger-marbles were carefully painted.
No fly could dare land on without slipping.

The shoes that she put on
That day had helped her
Grow taller seven centimeters.

I saw her walking fast
And as she passed I asked her:

Where are you going to, Pongo?
Why are you going too fast, Pongo?
Pongo, what's happening?

But she dared not stop as she glanced at me.
She passed as if the old mouth
That was talking did not exist.

Two spiky restive horses were riding her chest.
The two rebellious animals were agitated
As if they were burning from inside
And needed the action of some strong firefighters.

Her buttocks were swinging and dancing
Like the tail of a dog approaching its master.

I called her insistently; I called!
I screamed until I felt pain in my brain,
I screamed until my heart muscles got weaker.
But she dared not stop as she glared at me.

She passed like one in a big hurry
That might be taking some offertory
To the ancestors or to the gods
To save a life in serious danger.

She laughed sulkily and went uncaringly,
She went as though I did not exist.
I insisted, I insisted as she went like rapids:

Pongo, now I understand that you won't stop.
You won't stop and listen to me unless
Those spiky horses genuflect to the time.

Pongo, you won't have ears to listen,
Before some young males' hands and lips
Turn into firefighters and passionately
Put off the fire on those horses on your chest.

Ah Pongo, you won't stop and listen to me,
Before young bees search, find and sting
The fresh flower that nestles in your fork,
Harvest and harvest that fresh juicy flower.
Pongo, ah Pongo, Pongo!

In Pongo lurk many things and nothing,
Nothing…
She is a big mountain,
A big mountain of sand
That twinkles on the hurricane's way.

Young and naïve like a child,
Beautiful and transient like desert flowers,
Strong and brief and weak like a big torrent,

Amazing and precious like an old treasure,
Secret and evanescent like a profound pleasure,
Apparently she's everything, and nothing.

Ah my poor Pongo, Pongo!
At that segment of life,
At the moment when those horses
And that flower savor the spring of life,

At that section of the life's stream,
At that very dangerous age,

The mind and the ears of young folks
Hate the nutritive seeds of moderation,
Reaped and shared by the wise souls of the world.
They embrace and love Exaggeration.
They love their decisions which are destructions.

Our fights for freedom

Why do we remain behind, far behind?
Why do we remain here still like a pond?
Oh why are we here …here still?

We have walked; but not enough.
We have acted; but not right.
We have acted; but without intelligence and unity.
We have acted; but without enough strength.

Our efforts hang beneath the might
Of the forces which keep us in the chains.
Our fights for freedom have been torrents.

When these fights stop being torrents,
When these fights become permanent streams,
Streams that flow angrily and fiercely
And roar like the Nile River,

When they become permanent streams,
Streams which flow and scream bitterly
Like herds of elephants that fire
Some piercing warning whistles in the air,

Oh! At that time, we will have the Sun.
We will have it, we will have it.
We will reach the mighty land of freedom,
We will be free; we will be a free people.
We will bathe in the great waters of freedom.

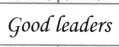

Good leaders

Good leaders. Who are good leaders?
concerned shepherds who firmly stand
and lead the cattle to the greenest pastures.

On my mind grows and streams
a long, long raging dream…
I dream of our people,
of our people led,
led by good leaders,
by good leaders; I dream,
I dream, I dream of it, I dream.

Our people have a lot of talents,
a lot of talents.
they are rich rainforest that contains
all kinds of plants,
of fauna, of gems and mines …
all kinds.

Our people have a lot of talents.
they are stronger than big rivers.
they are fertile like volcanic lands,
they are wonderful.

Our people have a lot of talents,
a lot of talents.
but they are held
and kept down
like the waters of some crater lakes.

our people are young plants,
young plants caught,
young plants strangulated,
strangulated by creepers.

From their leaders' faces and hearts,
there isn't any place for love,
there isn't any.

on their leaders' faces are but lit lamps,
lit lamps of indescribable hatred,
lit lamps of cruelties.

In those leaders' eyes grow
and flourish words
which cannot be bore
or be said by the people's tongues.

Inside those leaders
are roast minds,
minds that are on fire,
fire of hidden fears and tears.

Our people are a vast fertile land,
a wonderful land,
ah! which wind ever will drop on
the best of seeds?

Our people have a lot of talents,
a lot of talents.
our talented great people are due,
but where are the midwives?

Our talented great people are due,
and the midwives are busy;
they are distracted by something else.
our people fall down and cry, sob ...
but the faces of the midwives
are veiled in strong masks of indifference.

Our talented people are due,
but the midwives are nowhere to be found.
ah, chainsaw on my soul!

We climbed the tree,
And a wild lion came and sat under it,
how should we get down?
when should we be the masters of our life?
when should we have a peaceful life?

Across my chest pass some arrows of nostalgias,

across my chest pass some arrows of ire,

across my chest pass,

and pass the wild arrows of raw frustrations,

pass, pass and pass

some sparkling speedy arrows of killing pain.

As I stare at our people,

As I stare at our dear people,

our talented great people,

our crucified people,

the arrows of pain rejoice,

rejoice in my soul, in my chest;

rejoice, rejoice, rejoice …

help me, O Sky!

help me, O our Ancestors!

Young people today

Child,
Today,
Young people don't know the distance.

Child,
Today,
Young people sit too close to the parents.

Child,
Today,
Young people sit too close to the strangers.

Child,
In our days,
The distance was significant.

Child,
Today,
When young people listen to us,

Child,
Today,
When young people look at us,

We peep at the distance
And there is no distance.
In our days, distance was king.

Child,
Today,
When young people talk,

They are often noisy
Like dozens of donkeys
Braying and braying at the same time.

Child,
In our days,
Distance was the main rule.

Child,
Today,
Young people don't walk anymore.

Child,
Today,
Many years' walk is shortened to minutes,
And rapidly,
Youth's feet are full of thorns.

Child,
Today,
Young people sit too close to the parents,
Young people sit too close to the strangers.

Child,
Today,
Young people don't know the distance anymore,
They don't care about distance anymore,

And they are paying the price;
Everywhere they are paying the price.

Child,
As you see,
Young people are falling down,

Child,
As you see,
Young people are falling down,
Falling down, falling down; falling down!

As you see,
Young people are falling down,
And they need some hands to get up.
And they need more hands to get up.

Child,
You see, it's a disturbing actuality,
It's a serious situation
On which less attention falls,
On which nobody seems to bother.
Nobody, nobody,
Nobody.

Before we met

Before I met you,
My mind was as calm as well water.

Before I met you,
My sleep was as deep as the baby's sleep.

Before I met you,
My face was a lit bright lamp.

Before I met you,
My eyes were dry and bright
Like the smile of a cotton field.

But look, look at me today!
Do you remember me?
Can anyone do?

Do you remember that time?
That time, that idyllic time…
Do you remember it?

But look at me today!
Look at me, look at me.

To me,
You were Innocence.
You were an earthworm.

To me,
You were an earthworm, indeed.
You were an earthworm.

You were it,
Until the day ... the day ...
In your mouth I discovered the venom,
The venom there, abundant
In your sweet juicy mouth ...

I thought I was sleeping,
I thought I was dreaming,
But I was wrong, really wrong.

When some questions fought
And found their way
Out of my ire and tears,

Not a single drop of remorse
Crossed your windows;
I looked at you,
Your eyes ran away.

A wave of winged silence followed.
It was all, and until now.

My discovery opened me the door
And now ... now,
I know more sad things about you.

I know your parents.
I know their lives, their hearts;

I know a lot about them,
I almost know all about them:

They are truthful and sensitive,
They are kind and trustworthy,
There are peaceful folks,
They copiously care about each other.

As I think about them and look at you,
As I see their lives and glance at yours,
I remember some of my village's sayings:

The wasp's often begotten by the bluebottle,
The earthworm sometimes begets the boa,
The eagle at times comes from the sparrow's nest.

After the harsh autumn,
Plants' roots remain in peace.
After the harsh cold season,
Trees and grass recover.

After the fire's visit in the wilds,
Peace comes back,
And new lives begin again,
And new faces smile again.

At this moment, rebellious winds
Keep going like an army of crabs.

At his crossroad,
Which direction may I take?
Like this nature,
When am I going to recover?

Dreams, dreams!

Dreams, dreams!
Dreams, O life's strong incentives!
Dreams make life stream so quiet,
So good that burdens turn lighter.

Dreams, dreams!
As dreams come true like a river
That goes to sleep in the sea,
New dreams must be lit to keep life lighter,
Keep it lighter than butane gas in the air.

Dreams, dreams!
When life has no dreams to hold onto,
When life has no dreams to hug jealously,
When life has no dreams to caress,
When life has no dreams to feed on,
She becomes too heavy to be lifted daily,
She is heavier than all the steels
Which support the Wouri Bridge.

Dreams, dreams!
Dreams are to life what drums
Are to a traditional African dancer.
They bewitch us,
Yes they bewitch us,
And we know no night.

They make us move,
They make us run,

We get drunk over them,
And we jump,
Jump, ignoring the rain,
Jump scorning bad fates,
Jump resisting the cold,
Ah! We jump, we jump,
Jump challenging raging fires,
Jump defying the floods,
We jump, we jump,
We jump, and jump and jump.

Dreams, dreams!
Any dream that enters its harbor
Always arrives with happiness.
But it doesn't last.
It is just for a short while.
Thus we must be very careful.

Any dream becoming true
Can turn to be life's killer,
If life like a hungry leech does not
Hastily find a new dream,
A new dream to cling on,
A new dream to feed on,
And move on
To find again a new dream,
A new dream,
A new dream to cling on,
To find again a new dream,
A new dream,
A new dream to feed on.
Dreams, dreams!

Water's teeth

The water opens largely its silvered teeth,
It rushes into its banks,
Violently attacks and bites them
And goes back carrying some bits of flesh;

The banks see the executioner go and come.
The banks see him go and come.
They think he'll stop,
But he keeps going.
The banks whisper to the aggressor:

Water, strange being, what is all this for?
You always sow violence and don't know
Or say any word of love and friendship.
Water, strange being, what is all this for?
Water, you don't know moderation.
That's sad. That's very sad.

Water, I know how bad your ears are,
And you shan't listen to me
As I tell you that you ardently dig your own grave.
Water, yes you do. You do
Water, water! Lo! Ah, lo!

We, the banks, are parents protecting children.
We are the lips that cover the teeth.

If children choose to destroy their parents,
If the teeth choose to eat up the lips,
Isn't stabbing themselves in the chest?
Isn't it committing suicide?
Isn't a clumsy step to finish down?

Water, O expeditious sacrifice!
Water, cut our throats and gnaw at our lips!
Gnaw and gnaw at our lips!
Keep busy... destroy your protectors!

Water, and when you finish your sublime task,
Understand that you'll not sleep anymore.
You'll have no bed to sleep in anymore,
You'll scatter all over forever,
You'll have no strength anymore,
You'll have no smile anymore.

Water, water, water where is wisdom?
Water, water, water where is moderation?
Ah water, keep on us your stormy teeth!
With your vicious steels tear our lips out.
Don't sleep water, don't sleep water.
Water, don't rest, don't rest, don't rest...
Water, water, go! Go far, go far and get lost,
Get lost in the house of total wretchedness.

Is it the twilight of humankind?

Forebears, I come …
I come to you because I am lost.
I come to you because I am lost.
I have nowhere else to go, forebears,
And come to you, to you, to you.

I come to you because I want to know,
You are the only ones,
You are the only ones that can know it.
Forebears, forebears,
Is it the twilight of humankind?

We light up our lamps,
We write a lot,
But many eyes don't read.

We light our lamps,
We talk seriously,
But many ears don't listen.

We light our lamps,
We point at many life's traps,
We point at deadly abysses,
But many people walk and fall into them.

We light our lamps,
We open many umbrellas,

73

We give away many raincoats,
But many people get wet.

We light our lamps,
We put marks on the shallow
And rocky places of the waters,
But human boats go
Collide there and capsize or sink.

Thunders send warnings to men,
But rain comes down afterward
And they seriously get wet
And torrents end up carrying them away.

Forebears, I come, I come
To talk to you because we cannot
See our own back.

Forebears, forebears!
What had happened to humankind?
What happens to humankind?
I would like to know,
I want to know,
No!
I need to know.

Children don't want to listen,
Children don't want to grow up,
Adult don't learn from their falls,
And the poignant thing's that
Most of the elderly are dying young.

Forebears, forebears!
Is it the twilight of humankind?
Forebears inspire me, O inspire me!
Forebears, because I know you know,
I come to you, I come to you.
O Inspire me, inspire me.

Money and friendship

Money lands on our hands and flies away,
Lands and flies away; lands and flies away.
We earn it and spend and earn it again.
We win and lose, lose and find.

The airport of friendship's different,
It is different from the airport of money.

When we earn friends and spend them,
We may not earn them back again.
And those of them we earn back
Look like plants beaten and bent by storm.
Those friends are never the same again,
They are never the same again.

Good friends are not money we win and spend.
To earn and keep good friends, we must first
Learn the art of always treating them well.
O you, to prevent good friends
From leaving the airport of friendship,
Master the art of treating them well.

Under escort, at last it penetrated Abidjan

That year, Ivory Coast was a big stage.

That land became a big stage,

A big stage where was thrown the world bias,

A stage that hosted the world duplicity,

A stage that hosted the world insanity,

A stage that hosted all the world cruelty,

A stage that showed a divided people;

Ah! how shall it be forgotten?

Resolutely, something was coming to Abidjan.

It wasn't a safe but it looked like one.

It looked like a safe that was made in Paris,

It looked like a safe that was assembled in Burkina,

Was overtly polished by Washington and the UN;

Ah! how shall it be forgotten?

It wasn't a safe but it looked like one.

It was something heavy and costly to those

Who were sustaining or bringing it.

It wasn't a safe but it looked like one.

It was a special huge-heavy democracy,

Heavier than the heaviest of saves;

It was coming from the former master,

To butcher the one conducted by president L.G.

Previously dispatched in Ouagadougou,
It passed the boundary easily,
And entered the north of Ivory Coast,

But it was very tough to bring it to Abidjan,
And for many years, it wandered desperately
In the north of Ivory Coast among the populations,
Clinging onto the night, sowing suffering,
Spreading pain and causing many, many deaths.
Ah! how shall it be forgotten?

As G.S.' men couldn't enter Abidjan,
In long years they looted the country's wealth,
They plundered the country's wealth,
They plundered and plundered
And sold them on the black market,
And overnight, a desert neighboring country
Became a great producer of cocoa;
Ah! how shall it be forgotten?

As G.S.' men couldn't enter Abidjan,
They forced people to work for them,
Day and night they forced them to work.
Those who dared say, No, were seen
As the enemies of the new democracy
And were beaten, beaten and slain.
Ah! how shall it be forgotten?

Put on its way to Abidjan,
That democracy was a huge heavy save

Placed in a big lorry,
And protected by armed forces
Under the control of the former comrade, G.S,
(A good puppet, the kind that the West loves)
It was Ivory Coast nastiest year of democracy.
Ah! how shall it be forgotten?

To help themselves, France,
The former master, and Washington-UN,
All together were helping a former IMF official
With that special democracy to enter Abidjan;
Ah! how shall it be forgotten?

The armed forces escorting democracy
To Abidjan reached Douékoué,
The impostors were not welcome at all,
Its inhabitants looked down on it.
They did reject it, they hated it.
They were then seen as a big threat,
They were seen as threat to the lions' meals.

Ah! yes Ivory Coast was the lions' meals.
After Ivory Coast elections, Paris
And Washington declared A. W. the winner.
People,
Where did this happen before in the world?
Nowhere, nowhere…

President L.G., the man of peace, the sheep,
Bleated: in this country, we need peace.

We must avoid useless bloodshed.

People, let us recount, let us recount.

After the recount if I were the looser,

I will step down; I will go. Let us recount.

But Paris said, no. Washington said, no.

UN said, no.

A.W. said, no; I am the winner.

As democracy was taking time

To reach Abidjan and its House,

The French army stormed the Palace,

Seized the leader in power

In order to facilitate the coming

Of the new Child;

Ah! how shall it be forgotten?

In the streets of Abidjan,

The supporters of the new democracy

Chased and arrested unarmed young protesters,

They undressed them and here and there,

They placed a bundle of five, ten or fifteen men

On the grass or amid the roads and say,

'Be nice; you'll be fine.'

Then, all of a sudden,

'Bo bo bo! Boom, boom boom…

Peeef peeef… crack crack crack!'

Ah! how shall it be forgotten?

Opened chests… red wine,
Opened heads… red wine, white cream,
Opened stomachs… last meals everywhere,
Broken limbs… red wine, with cream …
Poignant scenes, incurable wounds,
Ah! how shall it be forgotten?

That new democracy demanded a lot,
It asked a lot from the people of Ivory Coast,
Ah my brothers and sisters slain like pigs.
That new democracy sew chaos,
It got a lot from the Abidjanians.
Ah! how shall it be forgotten?

The new democracy cleaned up the Douékouans.
Women were undressed before the children,

Women were humiliated before the children,
Women were killed before the children.
Ah! how shall it be forgotten?

Girls were humiliated before the parents,
Girls were killed before the parents,
Women, children and almost
All the boys and men were burned or shot,
Babies too were burned, shot, killed.
Ah! how shall it be forgotten?

The new democracy cleaned up the Douékouans.
Houses and churches were looted,

Houses and churches were burned down.
Men and women who found strength
And fled to the forest were caught and slain.
Ah! how shall it be forgotten?

Ah, humans did this to humans!
Yes they did; yes it happened in Ivory Coast.
Such courage and madness solely exist in humans.
Such courage and madness
Do not exist in any beast in any bush on earth.
No, O noooo…!
Ah! how shall it be forgotten?

As the French soldiers with some armed criminals
That protected the new democracy toured the area
Smilingly and got rid of the bodies,
Making sure none of them was playing the dead,
They came across two strange corpses.

The strangeness wasn't on the bodies
Of the two boys,
The strangeness wasn't in the age
Of the two male children,
The strangeness was in the positions
And signs displayed by the two boys.

The mouths of the two children were open
As if they were still saying in French, 'You'.
Between them was a piece of paper.

On the face down was the map of Africa,
And on the face up the map of France.

The two children's lifeless eyes were turned to it.
Each of them had a finger
Pointed at the map of France.
One of the boys' feet was lifted
As if to tread the map.

As the busy soldiers stared
And stared inquiringly at the two bodies,
Some of them (born in Ivory Coast)
Surprisingly moved back quickly,
The French asked to know why.

They were told that the two children
Overtly were accusing and cursing France,
And were guaranteeing that sooner
Or later, France would seriously suffer
From what was taking place in Ivory Coast.

One of the French soldiers stepped back
And pointed the gun at the two corpses…
(Guess what happened; guess what.
Unbelievable, unbelievable; ah unbelievable)
When he stopped,
There was but a ground red meat on the ground.
Ah! how shall it be forgotten?
Please tell me.

How shall it be forgotten?
Tell me. Please tell me how if you know.

Together, they all kept busy,
They toured and toured the large area,
Loaded their trucks,
Went and came back,
Loaded their trucks,
Went and came back,
Went and came back,
Went and come back …
Ah! how shall it be forgotten?
Please tell me.
How shall it be forgotten?
Tell me. Please tell me how if you know.

Long live new democracy,
Long live Ivory Coast
Nastiest year of democracy,
O darkest of crimes in the darkness!

Almost all the human rights activists
From the west were present at the scene
Like water in the Sahara.
Ah! how shall it be forgotten?
Please tell me.
How shall it be forgotten?
Tell me. Please tell me how if you know.

All this time,

The western Medias became aphonic.

Almost all of them became aphonic.

O darkest of crimes in the darkness.

It was Ivory Coast nastiest year of democracy.

Ah! how shall it be forgotten?

Please tell me.

How shall it be forgotten?

Tell me. Please tell me how if you know.

O Democracy!

Democracy, the right horse for business,

Human rights, the best bridge to business,

Democracy and human rights,

Excellent Trojan horse,

Soft paths to nations' dominations

Trojan horse for nations' looting!

Ah! how shall it be forgotten?

Please tell me.

How shall it be forgotten?

Tell me. Please tell me how if you know.

Today, the business that stinks has its master key:

Disrespect for human rights.

The business for the other nations' dominations

Has its master key:

Democracy; the hypocrite vile democracy.

Ivory Coast, O Ivory Coast of yore!
For power and business,
A peaceful nation became unrecognizable,
Completely unrecognizable.

For power and business,
A peaceful nation was turned into carrion
By a handful of local and alien hyenas-gangsters;
And as they keep sowing injustices,
And as they keep moving around and kill,
Kill and kill,
How shall it be forgotten?
Tell me. Please tell me how if you know.
Ah! how shall it be forgotten?

Ivory Coast my Ivory Coast,
Ivory Coast,
Generous, gorgeous young lady of yore,
From your ashes you shall be reborn,
Ivory Coast, dear land of my dear Africa:
From your ashes you shall be reborn.
Ivory Coast, you shall be reborn.
Ivory Coast!
Ah, those days, those chilling days!
How shall all that be forgotten?
How, how shall that be forgotten?
Ah! How, how shall that be forgotten?

In our daily life

In our daily life in our lifetime,
We live because we have to be,
We live because we have to be,
We live because we have a life,

A life to live,
A life we like to live,
A life we hate to live.

In our daily life in our lifetime,
We live for a strong reason,
We live for a shameful poor purpose
Or we live just to live,

We live a colorless life,
We live with joy,
We live without joy,
We live with sorrow.

In our daily life in our lifetime,
We live a full life,
We live half a life,
We live an empty life,

Whether it is a full, half or empty life,
We all live with death,
Constantly with death,
Too close to death.

No matter the fullness of our life,
No matter the vacuity of it,
No matter how longer we live,

We live with death,
From our first seconds,
From our first day to the last,
We live with death;

We live in joy or pain with it,
It gives blows here and there,
It blossoms and follows us everywhere,
Just like the air we daily breathe.

But we must not give it a big seat,
We must not have a seat for it in our life,
We must even keep it away,
And live fully the life we have.

The raped and the rescuer

Here and there in the valley, on the hills,
The trees' torn clothes remained scattered,
And that reminded us what the rapists
Had done to them in the recent months.

Here and there on the landscape,
The naked raped whistled and whined,
The naked raped whistled and whined,
They whistled and shouted at the invisible visitor:

–Shame, shame on you! Shame on you!
Stop doing all that to the innocent ones.
Shame, shame on you! Shame on you!

Last season you came and for your pleasure,
You took off all our clothes without our consent.
You humiliated us; you put us naked, naked.
You are here, you are back again,
What do you want, what now do you want?

Ugly and empty as we are, what now do you want?
There is nothing to steal from us anymore.
Go somewhere else and show enmity.
Go somewhere else and sow cruelty.

There is nothing to steal from us anymore.
You did everything last season,
You got everything last season.

Shame, shame on you! Go back!
Parasite, go back; go back, go back.
O go sow cruelty somewhere else!

–No, ladies, there is misidentification.
I am a good man, I am not a rapist.
Humiliated ladies, feel my hands!

Feel my hands! They are not cold.
Feel my hands! They are not harsh.
My hands are soft and tepid.
I am here for you. I am here to help out.

I am not here to hurt,
I am here to fix, to fix
All damages to you done.
I am here to help,
I am bringing you some new clothes.

–Liar! We cannot swallow your soporific.
We have hear enough,
We have seen enough,
We have had enough.

–I am the hand that revives,
I am here to revive, I am here to heal.
I am bringing you some new clothes,
Some flowered clothes,

I am bringing back birds that will decorate
Your house with nests, eggs and kids,
I am bringing you some winged beings

That will celebrate your beauty
And eternity with chats and songs.

I am bringing you all your friends:
Soothing rain rich in sodium,
Butterflies,
Dragonflies,
Honey-bees,
Cicadas …

I am bringing you some ants
That will rid you of greedy-vampire caterpillars.
I am here to repair.
I am here to heal,
I am the lavish hands of the lavish spring.

–O welcome, messenger! Welcome!
Some are here on earth to hurt or break,
The others wander after them to mend.
Welcome, messenger! Welcome!

Thus is life.
Welcome, messenger! Welcome!
You cannot imagine how happy now we are.
We are happier, the happiest.
But we are just tailless dogs.
O welcome! Welcome!

Death certificates

The death certificates described
That they died from cholera,
But it wasn't true,
It wasn't true.
They were masterly killed by someone.

The death certificates showed
That they died from malaria,
But it wasn't true,
It wasn't true.
They were steadily killed by someone.

The death certificates pointed out
That they died from sleeping sickness,
But it wasn't true,
It wasn't true.
They were carelessly killed by someone.

The death certificates announced
That they died from aids,
But it wasn't true,
It wasn't true.
They were coolly killed by someone.

The death certificates indicated
That they died from heart attacks,
But it wasn't true,
It wasn't true.
They were skillfully killed by someone.

The death certificates specified
That they died from cancers,
But it wasn't true,
It wasn't true.
They were proficiently killed by someone.

The death certificates were clear
That they died from cars accidents,
But it wasn't true,
It wasn't true.
They were expertly murdered by someone.

The death certificates said
That they died from gunshots,
But it wasn't true,
It wasn't true.
They were negligently killed by someone.

The death certificates detailed
That they died from skins burn,
But it wasn't true,
It wasn't true.
They were haughtily killed by someone.

The death certificates explained
That they died from respiratory diseases,
But it wasn't true,
It wasn't true.
They were deliberately killed by someone.

The death certificates testified
That they died from meningitis,
But it wasn't true,
It wasn't true.
They were serenely killed by someone.

The death certificates said
That they died from starvation,
But it wasn't true,
It wasn't true.
They were wolfed down by someone.

The death certificates concluded
That they died from poison,
But it wasn't true,
It wasn't true.
They were sturdily slain by someone.

The death certificates showed
That they died from violence and suicide,
But it wasn't true,
It wasn't true.
They were knowingly slaughtered by someone.

They were children, innocent children,
They were men and women,
They were adults and elderly.
One person killed them; all of them.

One person that is not apparently bad
Has harvested all those lives;
One that is even said to be kind,
To be innocent and generous still kills them.

The evil that is called State slaughtered them.
The government through its politics mowed them.
From the government-shield, the president killed them.

The president killed all those people,
This head of government killed them.
Ah president! Unworried piece of ill-luck!

And the people thought the president fought for peace,
And the people wanted things that way,
And the people praised the president for peace.

What about that silent war, all those crimes?
People's eyes oftentimes see short.
People are often victims of massive crimes,
But neither have they seen them nor the executors.

People oftentimes are completely blind.

People welcome their executioners,

People willingly follow their executioners,

People smile at their executioners,

They eulogize their executioners,

They play and drink with their executioners,

They pray and eat with their executioners,

And together with their executioners,

(These happiness-takers, these soul-takers)

People go and look for the source of their crises.

And together with their executioners,

People work to fix their broken lives.

Hand in hand they go and look for the killers.

O people, wake up! Wake up!

Not knowing each other

Not knowing each other, they met.

They met and met

And thought enough

They knew each other.

They thought they did.

They strongly believed they did.

They thought for sure they did.

They were living away from one another,

And that hurt them; that hurt them a lot.

They decided to live under the same roof then.

Not knowing where they were going,

They thought they perfectly did,

And went ahead and started the trip.

Amid the waves of passion,

Amid the strong harmattan of blindness,

They first called it love,

Then could not know what it was.

As they saw each other all the time,

Saw each other day by day, day by day,

As they stayed together and closer,

They felt far, far away one from another.

The gap they had tried to close widened,

The gap widened, widened and widened.

The situation got very bad, very bad.

The situation worsened, worsened.

Alas in the end,

What they had named Love ended up in hatred.

It ended up in raging river of hate.

It rolled from the mountain to the swamp,

The river of filth went from the continent to the ocean.

What faster brought them together,

What they first called Love and believed in,

That rapidly ended up in raw hatred.

That love, that love …

O no, no! It was something else.

Sure, it wasn't love; it wasn't love.

Lovers never got there. It wasn't love.

True lovers never got there.

What was it then?

What was that?

Ah people can call it what they want!

But it wasn't love; it wasn't love.

To Enoh Meyomesse

Enoh Meyomesse!
I saw your picture as you were a free wanderer,
And recently as you arbitrarily became prisoner.

The flute of jail has blown harder on you,
The flute of jail has carved
Its indelible songs on your face,
And darkened your sparkling eyes of yore.

Enoh Meyomesse!
Away from your family, from your friends,
Kept in the night in our dark country,
It is poignant, it is appalling; but listen!

An intellectual or a poet is not a peacock.

A caged plucked peacock loses its beauty,
A caged plucked peacock squawks lesser
And lesser and falls sick
For being tamed and naked,

A caged plucked peacock's squawks
And bawls are suffocated by deep sorrow,

A caged plucked peacock sinks into despair,

A caged plucked peacock collapses
From being caged and naked,

Enoh Meyomesse!
A caged intellectual or poet is not a peacock.

A caged intellectual or poet's beauty is his thought,
His belief, his courage and faith,
As he's forced to lie down in the rough days.

Enoh Meyomesse!
In the life of an intellectual or a poet,
An ill-luck can become a great propeller.

Enoh Meyomesse!
Our treasured country's a sheepfold
That is ruled and monitored by the lions.

The road to freedom is long and full of perils.
If there isn't justice for you now
In this confused dark part of the world,
Don't bend. Think, write and feed on hope.

If they choose to keep you there,
(What they'll probably do)
Keep yourself busy and don't give up hope.

And, who knows!
One of these mornings or noontime,

One of these evenings or night time,
Who knows!

From a group of elated patriots you could hear:
"Enoh, you and the others, wake up! Stand up!"

And as your heart beats at the speed
Of a hummingbird's wings in flight,
A struggle takes place in your assailed mind,

"These ones don't have guns"
"What is going on?"
"Is it the last moment?"
"Are they taking me to the stocks?"

With a great sun on their faces, they continue:

"Follow us! It is dawn, a new era."
"Come here! He's gone. The Shame is gone!"

And weakened and tottering, but smilingly,
Outside you'd join the patriots and sing:

"O freedom!"
"At last on the path of freedom here we're!"

Enoh Meyomesse!
Don't bend. Don't give up hope.
An intellectual or a poet is not a peacock.

As one people

As one people we must stand together,

As one people we must stand together

And say firmly,

"What matters most isn't what happened,

What matters most isn't what happened.

At this moment, our thoughts must be elsewhere,

At this moment, our thoughts must be elsewhere.

What matters most isn't what happened,

What matters most isn't what happened.

There is something better than it,

There is something better than it.

What matters most is what is happening,

What matters most is what is happening,

What matters most is what will happen,

What matters most is what will happen,

After all that had happened."

As one people we must look in this direction,

As one people we must stand together.

Bushy words

Like puppies whose parent is back from hunting,
They jump and talk with excitement:

Did you hear all those words?
That is the person we've been looking for.
Now, we have the right one!

They jump and talk with excitement:
Now we have the right one.
We do have the right one.
They jump and talk with excitement.

The old man's eyes become the rocks,
His limbs become the rocks,
His whole body turns into a massive rock.

They repeat the words,
They repeat them as if they were programmed.
And now the man lifts up the eyes:

Whoever goes quicker tearfully comes back.
Whoever drinks hastily swallows the wasps.
You don't bless and trust the unknown?
Let the wind of the time blow

And throw in your nose
All what is hidden in those bushy words.

They do not give in.
The old man is a preacher in the desert.

The man continues:
Whoever goes quicker tearfully comes back.
Be very careful!
Whoever drinks hastily swallows the wasps.

The old man continues:
The children from those lips are well chosen,
The children from those lips are the best.
They are surely honeyed children.
But they might have some stings.
They are a bathtub fill with an unknown liquid.

The old man continues:
Those words might be the ringhals venom,
The ringhals, the ringhals venom.
Do not hastily let your mind bathe in.
They might be the ringhals venom.
Beware of the words! Beware!
Words are human's best shields and weapons.
Beware, beware of the words.
Words are villain clever warriors.

Horse-Africa

Horse-Africa,

Who are these people on your back?

Who are they, Horse-Africa?

Horse-Africa,

Who are these people who ride you?

Who ride you to run over your children?

Who are they?

Who are they, Horse-Africa?

Horse-Africa,

Who are these people who ride you?

Who ride you and ride you to run

And run over your children and over?

Who are they?

Who are they, Horse-Africa?

Horse-Africa,

Who are these people who ride you?

Who ride you to set all these fires?

Who ride you to set all these fires?

Who are they?

Who are they, Horse-Africa?

Horse-Africa,
Who are these people who ride you?
Who ride you to provoke all these tears?
Who ride you to provoke all these tears?
Who are they?
Who are they, Horse-Africa?

Ah Horse-Africa!
Who are these people who ride you?
Ride you, ride you to fight
And wound Africans so deeply?

Horse-Africa,
This abuse will not last long.
This abuse will not last long.
Horse-Africa must be ridden for Africans.
Horse-Africa must be ridden by Africans.

Horse-Africa,
The damages are huge,
The damages are huge,
But this abuse cannot go on any longer.
This abuse cannot go on any longer.
O Horse-Africa!

The sky turned brighter

Last night I had a dream.

I viewed the sky turn suddenly brighter.

In the sky I viewed a huge door.

It opened itself broadly.

And as the sky shone intensely,

I viewed two men appear,

I viewed them come out

And descend onto earth.

They were walking hand in hand.

I heard them,

I suspected who,

I knew them,

I approached them,

I spoke to them,

I touched them.

It was Jesus and Mohammed,

But it could be Kimbangu or Lumumba.

It could be Nkrumah, Gadhafi or Confucius.

It was Jesus and Mohammed.

They were on a great mission on earth,

They came to unify all the nations,
They came to pacify the world
And create the world's central government.

They came to wipe out worries,
They came to put an end to suffering,
They came to eradicate injustice,
They came to stamp out poverty.

The politicians told the two men
That the world did not want that.
The two men insisted to convince them.

Politicians told them
That it wasn't a miraculous task
And that they'd do it.

The two men insisted to convince them.
Politicians suggested elections
As the best way to settle the matter,
And the two men agreed to go ahead
And compete with our politicians for the w. c. g.

Politicians went and manipulated the peoples,
Politicians went and intimidated the people,
Politicians went and corrupted the peoples,
Politicians went and slandered the two men,
Politicians went and demonized them.

And henceforth,
People's views on the two men shifted,
People doubted of the two men's liability,
People regarded them as two evil men.

Elections went on.
Though it was known that
Politicians were impenitent wicked beings,

Though people knew politicians did not stand
And work for the world's betterment,

Though they knew that politicians did stand
And work for themselves and the wealthy hands,

They went voting and came back smiling.
When all the ballots were fairly counted,
The two men bitterly lost the elections,
And the world stayed on its path to darkness.

Politicians from all nations gathered.
They gathered and feasted, feasted ...
Feasted in honor of the Master of darkness,
They feasted and laughed and laughed.
They feasted and mocked the two men.

I jumped out of my bed confused
But I realized that it was just a dream.
I looked around and said:

It is just a dream, just a dream.
But thus is the world; thus is our world.
Thus is the world today,
Thus has become the world.

While people get drowned
And you hold their hands to rescue them,
If you are not cautious enough,

They can bravely bite you to bones.
They can valiantly take you under the water
As usually do the crocodiles.
Thus is the world; thus is our world today.

Leon Tuam

We became the hybrids of the changing world

They told us that we were in the night.
They insisted that we were in the night.
The majority among us trusted them,
Few among us talked of plot.

They asked us to embrace and marry the day.
We stood up massively and enthusiastically,
We left the night and embraced the day.

But once we had settled in the day,
We felt dizzy, we could not see.
We thought it was temporary,
We believed we would adapt.

Time passed and nothing changed.
Time passed,
And the day became darker than the night.
Time passed,
And we found out there was no sleep in the day.

After trying the two spouses,
After tasting the two worlds,
We could not move backward.
We could not move forward.
We merely became the hybrids,
We became the hybrids of the changing world.

Unsettled by my straight answer

That charming, caressing afternoon of July,
I was sitting on a bench in a recreation park.
My watch had stretched its tall hand,
And had firmly grasped twelve,
While it kept the short one on four.
In the sky, the eye of the day shone kindly
And softly as if it should not sleep that day.
As though it did not want to miss anything,
Not miss anything which took place on earth.
The firmament had taken off all her clothes,
And in her nakedness, her fullness and freshness,
She was a blue, gorgeous, young lady
Anyone would naturally fall in love with.

That charming, caressing afternoon of July,
I was sitting on a bench in a recreation park.
That day at that moment, women, men,
Children, plants and animals were carried,
Lulled and were under the weather's spell.

Here, children rolled up into the sand,
There, children sprawled in the lawn,
They ran, they jumped, and they played balls,
Or they had fun with their bicycles and tricycles.
From the benches here and there
As they chatted, chatted and chatted,
Many parents watched their children

Blasting the air with brighter laughter,

Filling the air with flashes of smiles,

Or with countless slow flows of words.

That charming, caressing afternoon of July,

I was sitting on a bench in a recreation park.

That day at that moment outdoor,

Pigeons flew quietly and patrolled the air,

Pigeons besieged the roofs, cooed and cooed,

From them pigeons watched and watched people,

Then cautiously they came down and neared them,

Turned and turned around them,

And would have to leave later only

When there was no food left on the ground.

Bees and butterflies wooed flowers here

And there and got drunk over them.

Some sparrows collected tiny grass seeds,

And at times in big groups would fly away,

Go and besiege some trees where in big groups

They'd have some gatherings and would warble,

Filling the air with songs and screams,

Flapping the wings noisily,

Flapping the wings disorderly,

And painting and decorating the air

With a fascinating dust of tiny feathers.

That charming, caressing afternoon of July,

I was sitting on a bench in a recreation park.

A little far away, far away from the spectacles,

A colony of tiny birds offered a show of their own.

They'd fly around and around making little noise

And forming a large, long belt or an arc, or a square…
Then suddenly, they would swoop down on a tree,
Would stay and stay there soundlessly, lifelessly,
And again they'd return in the air
And they would renew with the show.

That charming caressing afternoon of July,
I was sitting on a bench in a recreation park,
Engrossed in a paper on violence and war in Libya,
When an old, tall man who was out with his dog,
Slowed down as they approached me, and stopped.
The light on his face was the joy on the weather's.
We had a short, sweet talk about the weather,
But his greedy, big eyes all that time were skillfully
Stealing and devouring the paper in my hand.

I pushed completely at one side of the bench,
And he said as he sat,
"O my God! Libya is burning."
I nodded and added,
"Yes. The world has brought war to Libya."
"The world is pounding and pounding Libya."
He continued, "There're a lot of bad guys there now."
I replied, "Yes. But they weren't there before."
"The world has infested Libya with bad guys."
"And when I say the 'world' you understand."

His dog was very quiet, looking at me
Every time I talked, and at him when he did.
He continued, "Don't you think that those bad guys,"
"Or the ones in Iraq, in Syria or Afghanistan"
"One day might come and do the same thing to us?"

I looked into his eyes inquiringly and calmly.
He understood that I was questioning his words,
And he muttered, "I am sincere …I am sincere."
And I dropped, "Whether you are, or not,"
"Believe me, I have the answer."

He then adjusted his position as he waited for it.
The dog was watching us motionlessly,
As though it understood and learned from us.
When again I glanced at the tall, old man,
He did not even notice it. He had bent his head,
And was waiting for my answer
Like one at the court waiting for a sentence.

I looked at him again and poured,
"No hands from any afar land
"Will come and destroy America."
"No hands from any neighboring land
"Will come and take America down."
"I say no hands! I say no hands!"
"Only American people will destroy America."
"Only American people will take America down."
"I can assure you that they're already at work."

The light I saw on his face at the beginning,
Was at last replaced by a very dark cloud.
I had no doubt that he was an American patriot.
The conversation ended right there, and they left.
I felt that he was unsettled by my straight answer.

It was a wonderful day

I remember that day still.

It was a wonderful day.

That day is far behind me,

But I remember it still.

I can see it glance at me still.

I remember that day still.

I went back to live that day again,

But I failed.

Not getting discouraged,

I went back to live it again,

But I failed.

Went I decided to go back

And search for that wonderful day again,

I gathered the same ingredients

That once gave me that unforgettable day,

That once led me to it.

I woke up in the mood I had that day,

I wore the same clothes,

I ate the same meals

At the same places.

I took the same drinks
At the same places in the same cups
And the same amount;
It was in the same environment
Around the same faces.

It was at the same season,
The same day,
The same week,
The same month,
But of another year.

It was the same weather,
The same sky,
I followed everything.
I followed everything, step by step –
I did all I did in the past,
I said all I said in the past
To meet that wonderful day,
I did just what I did in the past,
But I failed.

I refused to give up.
I started all over
And that did not bother me.
I felt a great pleasure going back for it;
I even put more ingredients that time.
Again, I failed.

One trial, two trials … nine …
Nineteen trials …
I got tired,
I gave up and wondered:

Why did that day come into my life?
Why, if I would never find it again?

Now, with a wounded and resigned soul
Like a broken wing traveler bird,
I end up to this:

In the course of our life,
We have many days,
We have many months,
We have many years;

But in the course of our life,
There is only one unforgettable great day,
Only one unforgettable great month,
Only one unforgettable great year;

I remember that day still,
But I don't search for it anymore.
I've learnt to love any day I have,
I love any day I have,
And don't search for that day anymore.
No anymore, no anymore, no!

Story of my father and his visitors

I

The open-air place was a huge forest of eyes.
The face of the day was very clean and warm,
And the dance ceremony went on and on,
Without being crossed by any gap.

It was at that moment that I heard a knock.
I heard a knock at the door of my mind.
I ignored it and followed the ceremony,
I followed it as if I had heard nothing.

The knock echoed repeatedly.
I recognized the alien.
As I heard:

What did you do of the story?
That story must not vanish
Like mercury dropped on the dust.
Where is the story?

"To talk is to be understood.
Talk, please,"
I quickly poured down.

I talk of your father's story and his visitors
What did you do of it?

I said, "Come back later.
This is a wrong moment.
Remind me later on.
Come back when this event is over."

In an authoritarian voice the alien shot:
It is now!
Take care of it now!

It was as if some guns
Were unloaded into my brain,
I felt lost but did not give up,

"Look at this rainforest of faces!
What would they say and think about me?
It would be silly, outrageous and ridiculous.
Look at this sea of eyes?"

Don't be worried, the alien said.
Never be worried about the crowd.
You are the crowd.
You don't exist for the crowd.
Go ahead and eternalize your father's story.
Go ahead and put it down!

Not knowing how to persuade,
Not knowing what to say,
Not saying any word,

I retreated for few minutes
And casted some lines about the story
That pulled in my childish days.

II

My father's visitors used to swam over the compound
Like a colony of ants or bees as dawn hatched,
And swarmed out with the same swiftness
When from the height the planet earth's Nurse
Started giving people some soft harmless injections;

Other visitors would invade it
While the Nurse was going home,
And would leave after an hour or two.

One day,
One of the visitors stole a medicine and left.
It was a scarce product for many diseases
Such as,
Diarrhea, fever, migraine, heartburn, cough ...

When all the visitors got all they needed,
When they got medicine, advices and all,
When the house became our house,

My father said:

Son, one of them did a wrong thing here,

He pilfered a strong medicine here.

I saw him taking it and said nothing.

The man was well known around as

"Someone who makes things disappear."

And some tongues called him

"The superman who was born

With invisible magnetic in the hands."

Then my father continued smilingly:

Whether he uses or sells it,

It will not help …

It will not help him at all.

It is useless …

It will not help anyone at all.

I felt confused,

I felt that I had heard him with child's ear,

Then shyly I asked:

Is that strong medicine a wrong one?

No. It is a real, strong good medicine.

He has stolen solely a part of the whole.

Ah, ah! It will not help at all.

He has stolen just a portion of the medicine.

And where is the other part of it, father?

He looked at me and laughed noisily,
Like a river that is squeezed by the boulders,
And said: Son, stop being a child.

He lifted his finger and as it touched his lips,
He said repeatedly:
The other part of the medicine is here, here.
You see, son; it is here, here.
An important part of it is here, here ...

My father was a man I never failed.
I had always been up to his expectations,
He was always very proud of me.

But that day I noticed I was failing him.
From his face I sensed that it was happening.
It was better to move from dark to light
Than to remain in it for good; I said:

I don't understand, father.
I know I've fallen very low.
Please help me, father;
Help me to get it right.

O poor son, my son, don't do that!
Don't show me that all is gone when I am gone.
Today I am going to talk to you about life,
About this life, with its two faces.

III

He talked of the two parts of life:
The visible and the invisible;
He said both were equal, and added:

Last month, a dead man came here,
He asked for blood cleansing medicine.
We did not have it here.
Then he asked for cough medicine.
You took it and handed it over to him.
That dead man was smiling a lot.
He even gave you some gratuities.

I remember him,
Yes, I remember him, I see him.
He was not a dead person,
He was not a ghost.
I used to see him at the market place.
He looked very strong.
He looked happy and healthy.

I can agree. I partially agree with you.
The day he penetrated this house,
Already he was a broken useless calabash,
He was already a wandering cadaver.

O my father, how?
What is happening to you?

Nothing; nothing is happening to me.
What is happening is happening to you.
You are a chick and you must grow up,
Grow up quick, develop strong wings and fly.
Grow up quick in order to stop standing up
And jump from deep night to daylight.

As a ray of light took root in his eyes
And widened, widened and bloomed,
He said, as he stared worthily at me:

Before life fully slides away from a body,
The invisible part of life must run out.
The day that man was here, the invisible part
Of his body had already fallen apart.
At this point, nothing on earth can stand
And hold such a person back;
Nothing, son, nothing.

I felt sad for what would happen to the man,
Then, I went back to the stolen medicine
And the father almost thundered:

My son, ah my son,
With all these rains of words

Falling from my own mouth,
Don't you see where the missing part of it is?
What is that? I cannot recognize you.
My son, ah my son,
My urines are never stupid, never ever.

Look, son, what I always say here
When I give people medicine
Is as important as what they receive.
Sometimes I say it aloud,
But most of the time I murmur it,
Or just say it in thoughts.

And so are other true skillful hands
Vowed to this profession on our lands.

Without the words of that medicine,
The thief will not get all its benefits.
It is as if he has stolen solely one part
From a drug that has three.
The medicine he got is but a raincoat
Full of holes that one wears on a rainy day.

Son, very powerful are the words and thoughts
Of those who in moderation and purity live,
And bravely plow the spiritual garden daily.

Son, the invisible governs the visible.
The world is a bike with two wheels:

The visible wheel and the invisible;
To choose to ride only on one of them
Is but to get hurt, to hurt and fall down.

Son, to know a lot, don't talk a lot,
Learn to listen, learn to listen,
Listen to the right things,
Listen to the right voices.
Don't walk too much looking for knowledge,
You have a lot stored in you.
Dig, dig into yourself, and dig.
And son, don't forget:
Inside you,
There is what is out there.
Must of what is out there is with you, in you.

I know we are all important

Like busy bees in the garden, in the hive,
Any of us has a duty in this society.
Yes any of us does, we all do, we all do.

A good night watchman plays a key role
In the society as does a President,
A soldier, a doctor, a lawyer, a farmer …
I know we are all important.

My fellow,
With bravery and pride,
Carry out any of your daily duties.
Get them right, today and tomorrow.
I know we are all important.

In whatever you do, wherever you are,
Always give a sense to the life you live.
Be in control, and always be you.
I know we are all important.

Along the years
In this country, in that village, in this city,
People have told lies and lies;
Watch out, don't engulf them; be you.

Don't listen to them. Be you.
Do what you do. Nothing must shake
Or take away your convictions; be you.

Be a brain in control; be you.
And maintain this in your mind:

To see and rescue your society in collapse,
You don't need to be on a tall seat,
You don't need to be on the softest of seats,
You don't even need to be on a seat.

From an uncomfortable seat,
From a low seat,
From nowhere: a competent brave hand
Always must pull his land from disaster.

In whatever you do, wherever you are,
With bravery and pride,
Carry out any of your duties.
I know we are all important.

Don't let any wind grind you down,
Don't let any water-teeth eat
And wear away your great principles.
Be a brain in control; be you.
I know we are all important.

Do you see that child?

Do you see that child, that African child?
Do you see that child, that Palestinian child?

Do you see that child, that South American child?
Do you see that child, that Chinese child?

Do you see that child, that Indian child?
Do you see that child, that Afghan child?

Do you see that child, that Pakistanis' child?
Do you see that Congolese child, that Iraqi child?

Do you see that child, that Sudanese child?
Do you see that Syrian child, that Libyan child?

They are children,
They solely look like children,
But they are not children at all.

If you approach each of them graciously,
If you look at each of them lovingly,
If you talk to each of them caringly,
If you open the heart of each of those children,

You'll find in it a big deposit of suffering
That is scarcely found in the old man's heart.
You'll find in it a big deposit of suffering
That equals the volume of all Sahara sand.

If you open the heart of each of these children,
You'll find a land always rocked by the quake,
You'll discover in it many active volcanoes,
You'll view a farm hit endlessly by storms.
Around the head of each of these children
Shines a big crown of thorns,
A crown which is fifty times heavier
And spikier than the one that once
Was worn by a man.

Each of these children lifts a big cross,
Each of these children lifts a heavy cross,
Each of these children is a wretched,
Each of them is nailed on an invisible cross.

With all that had happened in these children's lives,
With all that is happening in their lives,
With all that will happen to them tomorrow,
With their woods of traumas
Which are known by their communities,
Which are known by their societies
And known by the whole hypocrite world,

Ah! How should these wounded children
Ever recover and become full men?
Ah, how should these wounded children
Ever recover and become full women?

With all these wounds,
With all these traumas,
I can only despise these known and unknown eyes
Who dare to foresee
Or talk of great future on the lands
Where stand these young wretched.

O astonishing strange children!
They run, they go and come.
They have jokes, they smile, they play…
They embrace everyone, they love everybody.
Their lives and survivals are but a miracle.
Their lives and survivals are full of mysteries.
They are children; but they are not children at all.

Life is adaptation

Life, life, life… life is adaptation.

Life, life, life… life is adoption.

Life is adaptation and adoption.

Any wise life knows that life is that.

An icy sea is not dead.

An icy sea is not a rock;

Beneath it is life aplenty.

Life, life, life… life is adaptation.

Life, life, life… life is adoption.

Calm water is not dead.

A leafless tree is not dead;

Inside it is life aplenty.

Life is adaptation and adoption.

Any wise life knows that life is that.

And any life that ignores that,

Any life that is rebellious to that,

Surely is doomed to wrecking.

Life, life, life… thus is life.

Life, life, life… thus is life.

Hundreds of years after those tragedies

Hundreds of years after those tragedies,
Those tragedies which unfolded on our lands,
Those tragedies which arrived like thieves
And weakened us as they built up the others,
O brothers and sisters, welcome home!

To come together as one people makes us stronger.
Who can deny today the dawn of a new era?
Who can say we are not advancing in some way?
O brothers and sisters, welcome home!

Gone centuries ago,
Gone with faces veiled in sadness,
Gone with bodies washed in tears,
Gone with fleshes fed on the lashes,
Gone with bodies covered with scars and sores,
Gone bleeding in the souls,
Gone bleeding in the vaginas,
Gone bleeding in the hearts, on the penises,

Living with fear,
Living abused and terrorized,
Becoming the floorcloth to clean the others
And make them shine like stars,
Living under unspeakable humiliations,
Living under people who owned you, the husbands,

Owned you, the wives; owned you, the children;
Living under frequent horrid punishments,

Living a life that wasn't life,
Living with death,
Living in death,
Suffering, learning, adapting;
Holding new tools and strengthening your power,
Adopting this and that on the wings of the time,
Obeying the masters often like donkeys,
Saying no and becoming defiant at time,
Fighting them and losing so badly often,
Fighting them and winning at times,
Brothers and sisters, you have survived.
You have stabbed destiny in the face.
O what a so long, long walk!
Time, time, brutal killer!

And now, you decide to see home.
You decide to make Africa your home again.
You are moving back home,
You are home; feel completely home.
Well-armed, miraculously you see home at last.

Brothers and sisters, at last you are home.
Seeing where you were and where you are,
What an amazing story!
What a moving story; what an appealing story.
Our heroes, it is historical; it is historical.
Time, time, O sweet healer!

Africa, some tongues roar that some heavy,

Icy rains are coming down on you.

Africa, some tongues trumpet that some heavy,

Stormy rains are coming down on you.

Do they only know what is —these days —going on?

Do they know about these changes?

Do they know about your new Diasporas?

Do they know about this new era?

Who do these tongues want to scare off?

Anyway, not us anymore, not us.

We are getting united,

We are getting stronger,

We are getting wiser.

Pessimistic eyes must know

That African sky looks brighter than ever.

They must know that our sky is full of stars.

O sisters! O brothers! Welcome!

Welcome, welcome, welcome home!

This is Africa your motherland,

This is Africa our motherland.

This Africa is yours, this Africa is ours.

Welcome, welcome, welcome home.

Everywhere, go!

Go and run into the landscape

And wallow or roll in the meadow

Onto the grass, on the sand!

Everywhere, go!

Go and roll on the leaves, go, go!
Go and do it, from morning to evening
Fearlessly, fearlessly! You are free, go!

Everywhere, go!
Oh go and walk and talk aloud
Along the rivers, aloud along the brooks,
Aloud along the shores,
And bathe and swim and play
As you want fearlessly! You are free, go!
Go! And savor our sweet African sun
Fearlessly, fearlessly; you are free, go!

O sisters, O brothers, welcome home!
Everywhere, go!
Go, oh go and start your businesses,
At the city, at the countryside, on the water, go!
But beware of the crooks!
Beware of the wicked minds!
They are everywhere here.
They are everywhere on earth.

Sisters, brothers, welcome home.
Let us put our strength together for a better Africa.
Let us put our strength together for a new Africa.
Let us together bite any curse to marrow.
Time, time, brutal killer!
Time, time, O sweet healer!

Sisters, brothers, Oh go, go and build anywhere
On this wonderful land of opportunities!
Go! And build your businesses wherever you want
And prosper and live fully, masterly;
And live fearlessly, fearlessly. You are free.
On this big Building Site,
Walk fearlessly; you are free.
Work fearlessly; you are free.
Together, let us make history.

Sisters, brothers, Oh you must know:
African land is softer and full of opportunities.
Africa is a vast Building Site waiting
For her good sons and daughters.
Together on the river-future,
We shall build strong bridges.

O sisters, O brothers, welcome home!
After all those years of separation,
Welcome home.
After all those years of long suffering,
Welcome home.
After all those years of homesickness,
Welcome home.
Let our priests and wise men bless you,
Let our priests and wise women wash you.

Africa is your home, O sisters!
Welcome home!
Africa is your home, O brothers!

Welcome home!

We are brothers, we are sisters,

Together we are, we are together.

We are together forever and ever,

And together forever we shall conquer.

Time, time, brutal killer!

Time, time, O sweet healer!

At this segment of the journey

At this segment of the journey,

At this point, our words, our appeals

Our acts and whishes all come to this:

When love hurts us,

Solely love can heal and save us.

When hate hurts us,

Solely love will surely heal and save us.

At the end of the day, love will always

Be at the center of everything, everywhere.

Love is the heart and is at the heart of all.

At the end of the day,

Wherever and whoever we're,

Whatever we've sown or reaped,

At the end of the day,

Solely love will surely heal or save us.

Printed in the United States
By Bookmasters